10 Steps to your
SUCCESSFUL
Small Business Start-Up

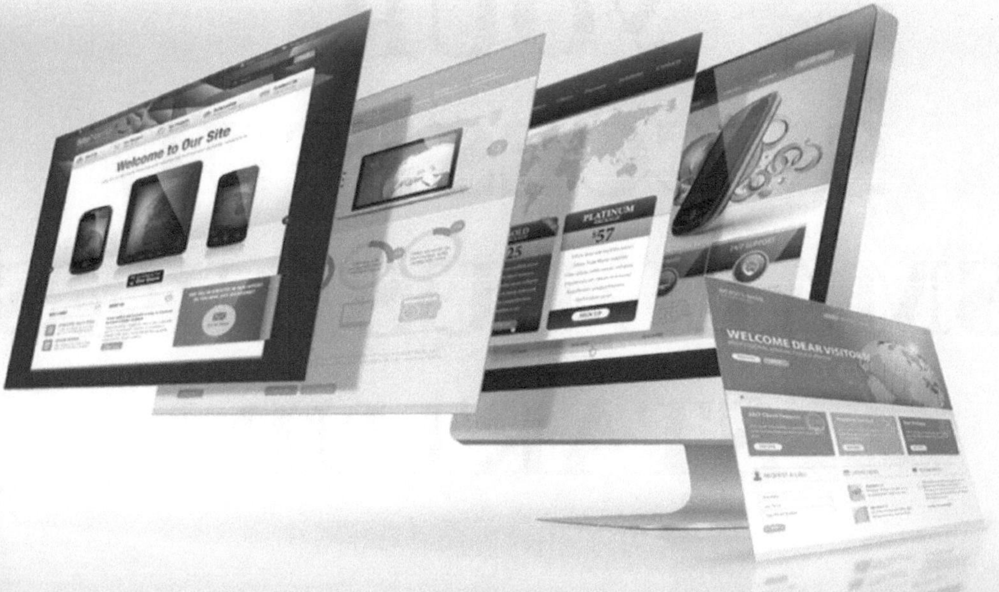

Irving Tryon

10 STEPS TO YOUR SUCCESSFUL SMALL BUSINESS STARTUP

Table Of Contents

INTRODUCTION

A lot of people mill around with the thought of starting a business which could be a great career or money making idea for themselves and their families at various stages throughout their lives, but there are many steps to starting a small business. Some reasons people look at this includes taking a break from work, health issues, down sizing because of the economy, or even just as a way to work from home and set your own hours. Contemplating the start up of a small business is simply the very beginning, but if you have moved forward with your idea and are taking the initial steps then there are a few things you should know about before you get in too deep.

DOMAIN NAME

Phone numbers used to be the thing. Business owners wanted phone numbers that were easy to remember - numbers stuck in a person's head.

What was the number for that plumber? Oh yeah, 555-1234.

Website domains have become the new phone number. And you're not limited to the numbers one through nine. With domain names, you have the ability to extend your brand and make it so much easier for potential customers to find, remember, and use your business.

As simple as it seems to pick a domain name - there are still a few important factors that you need to consider. Domain names are an extension of your brand, your business, you. They're also important tools that you can use to attract potential customers to your services.

Should I use my business's name?

This is one option to consider. It also depends on what your business's name is. If your business name is "Jacob and Sons Plumbing Services of Greater Miami" then you might want to consider another option. [http://www.jacobandsonsplumbingservicesofgreatermiami.com] is not going to fit onto business cards or the sides of trucks very well. Plus, when somebody is trying to remember your website, they might leave out an 'of' or an 'and' and then won't be able to get to the site.

Even if you're a Miami based plumber using the business name 'Jacob's Plumbing" you will want to consider a few things. http://www.jacobsplumbing.com might be available - but you'll want to think about how you are going to utilize your domain name.

Are you going to simply use it as a business card? That is, are you simply planning on marketing it in a way similar to that of a phone number? Hi, I'm Jacob. I'm a plumber, here's my website.

Or, are you going to try to market your business online in a way so that you are positioned strongly in the search engines for relevant keywords? That is, are you using the website to attract new customers from the internet?

There are ways to use your domain that makes it simple for people to remember, as well as increase the chances that search engines are going to rank your website highly for relevant keywords, like:

- Miami Plumbing Services

- Plumbers in Miami

- Local Miami Plumbers

- Local Plumbing Services in Miami

Not only is website content and keyword and phrase targeting important when it comes to search engine optimization, but domain names play a crucial role in search engine results rankings.

For this reason you should make sure you carefully consider all of your options when choosing your domain name. Figure out what purpose you want your small business's website to address.

- Is it an electronic business card?

- Is it an internet marketing tool designed to bring new customers to your business?

It's easy to try to just jump right into putting together a website - but before you purchase your domain, make sure you've taken the time to sit down and carefully map out your goals and needs for your business's website. Putting together a plan in the beginning will make the process go much smoother as well as make it easy for you to focus your site on your business's specific needs.

Invest in your website so that it will invest in your business.

EMAIL

Why You Need A Custom Email

When you launch a website, you want people to visit, check out your content, and engage with the site. In addition to social media and commenting, people also like to communicate and engage via email. When you have an email address that's not associated with your web domain, people are less likely to email you. It can also look unprofessional when you use email addresses like @gmail.com or @yahoo.com. Fortunately, you have another option, custom domain email. Here are a few of the advantages that come with having a custom email address:

1. Simplicity

When you have a custom domain email address, it is easier for people to contact you. Your audience will find your personalized email address easier to remember when they need it. As long as they know your domain name, they can remember your email address.

2. Credibility

People are more likely to engage with a website or company that has a custom email address. It makes you appear more official and better prepared to handle their queries.

3. Leadership

Everyone has an email address. Usually it's a gmail or yahoo account. You can set yourself apart with a personalized email address. Your custom email address also helps you increase brand awareness and demonstrate thought leadership. It makes you look more professional and well-established as an expert in your area of interest.

4. Consistency

With some email addresses like @comcast.net, you can't take them with you if you switch internet providers. You can maintain consistency and an appearance of reliability when you have a custom email address that you can take with you no matter what.

5. Personalization

With your custom email address, you can also create a variety of addresses based on your needs. For example, you can create one for each purpose or department that you have. If you're a business, you can create one for the billing, sales, and tech support departments. Or if you have a blog, you can create custom addresses based on the needs of your viewers like submissions@myblog.com or reviews@myblog.com.

No matter what kind of website you have, a custom email address to match your domain can help you achieve your goals.

PHONE

When somebody starts a business he or she can face many challenges along the way. The ups and downs may at times be so overwhelming that you feel weighed down. There are always potential challenges and you need to be savvy enough to get through them successfully. You need to look at ways that can help you and your business move forward and one of the more successful ways is Virtual Phone Numbers. Once explored, you can't ignore the benefits.

Personally, I do not think there is anything as effective as communication when it comes to business. If the communication channel is not properly utilised then failure looms. This is an area in which a company or business has to invest in properly for it to generate productive growth. In every company or business there are and need to be, authorities. They are put in at systematic levels and these authorities have ways of communicating. They provide instructions at different levels. These instructions are to be followed keenly by the subjects. Some instructions are urgent and have to be acted upon immediately. If the communication channel is slow then there will be a problem. So any business needs to ensure that communication lines are up to standard at all times.

Another feature that makes a business grow is open, consistent communication with consumers. When they feel you understand their needs, they will communicate back to you. Most consumers want clarification about certain issues and the need to have an easy way of reaching you without necessarily having to come in person. This can only happen if you have a clear, open line of communication.

When you have a Virtual Phone Number, customers can call you at a cost effective rate. It doesn't matter where your geographical location may be, your customers will be able to call you at their local rate. This gives them the feeling that you accessible and on call which can retain many customers. In reality you may be in a different state and time zone.

This technology is very good for small businesses. A newly born business will always want to grow, hopefully with rapid development. The fastest way to develop it is by utilising different communication channels. While it can help to gain more customers or clients, you will also be able to determine what areas of the business are more profitable.

However, it can be expensive setting everything up at once. This is especially true with a very young business and you may end up spending a lot of money in order to achieve this. On the other hand, if you want to create one line of communication up at a time then it can take you forever and cause the business to grow at a very slow rate. These two equations have to be properly balanced.

The easiest and fastest alternative is the Virtual Phone service. This allows you to operate your business in numerous locations without having to be there physically. Your consumers, while not knowing which area their calls are being received, will enjoy the benefits of calling you at their local rate. They will assume that you are in the same area as them and this is a factor that can also bring more clients into your business. It is a tool that has helped to develop many new businesses.

The way to do this is by using the right area code. By using the code as a prefix, it looks like a traditional number and callers assume they are dialling a conventional telephone number. You will then be in a position to do business in your areas of choice without situating a branch. This saves you a lot of money in terms of setting up and travelling. It also greatly increases your customer base. As it is a beneficial way of allowing your company to stay in touch with customers, this can speed up the growth rate for your business.

It is also possible for your friends and family to call at a 'friendly' rate from wherever you are. The calls can go through a computer and you can attach the virtual number to a conventional or cell phone. It will be easy for you to communicate with many people while giving them a sense that you are in the same area. There is no geographical discrimination and distance is never a factor.

Obtaining this technology is costly however it certainly isn't as expensive as setting up numerous branches in numerous locations. You will be required to pay an establishment fee and a small administration fee. There is also a monthly subscriptions fee. This is relatively small and depends on the rate at which you have used the service.

This technology is rapidly increasing in demand especially among small businesses so many companies are offering the service. Before deciding which one best meets your needs, read their terms and conditions thoroughly. Check all fees, terms and benefits they can offer your business by visiting their websites. You will be able to make a request online or alternatively, call them to get a complete break down of what they can offer you. This will save you time and money by having to go to their office.

If you are a small business just starting out, you'll definitely want to consider using Virtual Phone Numbers. It could make a big difference to your valuable business.

LOGO

If you are starting a new business, then you must be in the process of defining its processes and policies. If you have already launched your business, then you must be working on creating a powerful marketing strategy to give your business a significant push and make it widely known. I say, you are going in right direction. However, have you already created a quality logo design to represent your business? If not, then you need to hold your horses now and get a top quality custom logo design for your business as soon as possible.

"Is a logo really important?" You may ask.

Well, let me ask you a question now, "Have you seen any famous business without a logo yet?"

No one has, because there isn't any famous business without a logo. This is the reason why you should work on creating a top quality custom logo design for your business.

How do you expect your market to recognize you and your products? You may advertise one product in the beginning, but later you may have dozens of products. Through advertisement you will be able to make your first product famous, but how will your other products be recognized?

It's your logo design that will tell your market that you are the creator of the product. It means your logo gives your business a face through which people begin to recognize you and your products or services.

Also, those who don't know anything about your company, will judge your level of quality by looking at your logo design. If it will be of low quality, people will think that your products will be of low quality as well and, thus, they will pick up the products made by your competitors.

Getting a logo design is important and its importance can easily be witnessed if you notice how much money and time large businesses spend on creating a quality logo for their business.

Let's look at Pepsi's logo. Pepsi changed it not too long ago. Pepsi doesn't need any introduction, we all know about Pepsi, but they still changed their logo. This clearly shows that logo design plays a crucial role in terms of helping a brand become stable or grow bigger.

You can now very well imagine how important it is for small businesses to get a quality logo. If you want to compete with large organizations, then your logo can help you stand-out.

Now, there is one important thing we should discuss now. There is no need to feel intimidated that you will have to spend thousands of dollars in order to get a high quality logo. If this is the reason why you never thought about designing a logo before, then you made a big mistake.

Due to increasing competition in design industries, custom logo designs don't cost a fortune now. You can now get a top quality custom logo design at a fraction of the cost. With a little research, you will be able to find many affordable companies online.

BUSINESS CARDS

As more and more people are affected by the economic downturn, many are looking to cash in on their talents to make extra cash on the side. Others are diving in headfirst to start up their very own small business. And one key strategy to help jumpstart your business and maintain its growth is networking. Everyone doing business has to get their name and information about their product or services out there. A great way to do this is to have creative, effective business cards to leave with people you meet.

Creative, eye-catching business cards can be printed relatively cheaply. They are transferable, meaning that people tend to pass them on to others who might need your services. And, they make you directly accessible even if you haven't setup a website yet or created printed marketing materials. We will discuss how to visually enhance your business cards so that they do their jobs.

Do's and Don'ts to get effective, creative business cards,

DO:

1. Use your well-designed logo and display it prominently.

2. Make sure your company info is correct. Check and double check your name, position, company, phone and fax numbers, website, blog, tagline etc.

3. Tell people what you do. The card should describe your business and specify why they should do business with you, instead of your competition. Use both sides if you can afford it, so that you are not cramped for space. Plus, that's more prime real estate for marketing your services.

4. Design it. (Using a stock/template card will look just like everyone else's card.) You can easily do this yourself. Companies like Vistaprint allow you to upload your own design.

5. Better yet, hire a professional who will make sure the card is visually balanced and typographically pleasing.

6. Your card should reflect you. When appropriate, let your personality shine through, or give people visual cues about your skills.

7. If you want to splurge, some great ideas which include embossing, metallic, quirky, cutouts, odd shapes and sizes, translucent, popups, textured and more. Of course be careful as some of these wouldn't fit in standard business card holders. If most in your industry keep their contacts in a digital format or online, then go for it!

DON'T:

1. Use cheap paper. Buy the best you can afford.

2. Get free cards with a sponsor printed on the back.

3. Make type too big or too small or plaster it over a busy photo, rendering it completely illegible.

4. Place type too close to edge of the card. This screams amateur.

Follow these tips and you will be able to network effectively and leave a good, professional first impression wherever you go.

WEB HOST

When you are looking at making your own website, you will have to figure out what type of web hosting best meets your needs. There are several different types offered and each one comes with its own pros and cons, so you should educate yourself before making a choice in order to ensure you get what you need. The main types of web hosting that you can choose from are free hosting, shared hosting, dedicated hosting, windows hosting, and ecommerce hosting. In addition to look at what they offer, you also need to honestly ask yourself what you need from a web host.

- Free hosting is what many internet service providers offer their customers. It tends to have low storage and bandwidth limitations, but offers free email and is generally a good choice for a small, family and friends type page. This type of hosting is very limited, but offers a good solution for hosting a few images or practicing your web design skills.
- Shared hosting is the most common and least expensive web hosting option, aside from the free ISP hosts. It is quite simply that your website is hosted on a server that is shared with many other websites. It has higher traffic and bandwidth allowances than a free site, but tends to have a lot of restrictions and isn't as secure due to having many sites on one server. This type of host is ideal for small businesses or other sites that can expect average amounts of traffic.
- Dedicated hosting means that your website is hosted on its own server. This option is especially good for large businesses whose sites get a large amount of traffic. They often offer multiple domain names and email options as well as large database and software support. The downside to this type of

hosting is that it tends to be significantly more expensive and also requires a higher level of skill to create and maintain a site.

- Windows web hosting is meant to be used with Windows computers and software. If you don't use windows, then you'll have to find a host that offers support for operating system, such as Linux. It is important to get a host that supports your system because you won't be able to use your host to its full potential if you don't.
- Ecommerce web hosting is specifically meant for online businesses. These hosts generally provide you with a number of tools and packages that are specifically suited towards making an online business function, such as email packages as well as shopping carts, payment methods, and other options. This hosting option is good for cutting down on the hassle of making a business website.

You might be confused about your options at first because of how many there are, but as long as you take some time to carefully consider your needs, you won't have any problems. Once you've determined the type of web hosting that you want, you can start looking at individual sites so that you can choose the best one for you.

WEBSITE

These days, a business just isn't a business without a website. Customers have grown to expect the convenience of online access, even in industries where a web presence doesn't immediately seem necessary. Hair cutters, farmers, electricians - even mom-and-pop institutions need websites!

The good news is that, as websites have become more necessary, they have also become easier to create. This year, hundreds of thousands of websites will be created, many of them by the entrepreneurs themselves. In the past, web developers were a necessity in a world of HTML and PHP (web coding languages), but these days anybody can create a website. And you can too!

The first step is probably the most difficult, but you don't need a computer to do it! The first thing you need to do is to think about what your website should look like. Before you spend a lot of time constructing the face of your business, you should probably decide what your website's function will be.

Once you've determined what your website does, it's time to try to figure out a simple way to design your site to meet those requirements.

Let's think of a concrete example. Let's say we run a business that delivers fresh baked cookies to people all across Ottawa. What would you like our website to do? Well, a good function for a website like that might be to have a place where people can order our cookies from their computers or phones. That's a great purpose for our website, and I think people would appreciate not having to call to secure some of our delicious white chocolate macadamia treats.

Once you have the primary function (in our case, it's cookie ordering), you can structure the rest of the pages around it. In our example, let's make the main page the cookie order page, and make it so that other pages are accessible through the menu. We could have an "about" page where we talk about why we started the business. We could have a "location" page where people can find out where our store is. We could even have an "apply" page where people can try their hand at becoming cookie deliverers like us!

Now that we've figured out the basic operation of our website, it's time to start building! Don't worry! It's easier than it sounds, and if you make a mistake, no one will notice. Getting a domain is very essential and you can make use of platforms like wordpress and blogger. Though wordpres has more functions compared to blogger.

Once places for teenagers to create emotional personal blogs where they talked about how angry they were about their parents, blog creation websites have recently become one of the easiest and most powerful website creation avenues. WordPress is generally regarded to be the better of the two mentioned above, so try that one if you're just starting out.

WordPress lets you pick from a range of free themes, many of which are of a very high quality. If you don't find anything that works for your website for free, you have a couple options: pay for a premium theme, or modify a theme to better suit your needs.

Premium themes are available from places like Templatic. In some cases, you can even get a team of specialists to work on your design for you.

But if you want to go the free route, you're going to be in for a bit of a hard time. Modifying themes means learning a bit of coding (ew!). Think of it like renovating your kitchen. If you want to do it yourself, you're going to have to study some electrical charts (and probably take out life insurance). Remember, if you can find a free theme that works for you, just go with that!

You can learn some basic HTML at places like codecademy.com, or you can just plunge right in, stripping things out of the code behind the website until things work the way you want.

You might want to have a code-familiar friend on hand to help you. You know... just in case things get a little tense around the house.

Once you are done all of that, it's time to make it official. Start shopping for a host! My favourite is Servage, but other options, like Canada's Netfirms are also quite good. Find a pricing structure that works for you. For a small business, you're probably looking at an investment of about 50 bucks a year. That's nothing huge in the grand scheme of running a business. You'll probably spend more on cookie trays in a month!

SALES FUNNEL

When we first talk to clients they all seem obsessed with getting people to their website. They seem to think that by driving enough people to the website that some of them will stick. Sure, if you throw enough darts at the dart board you are eventually going to get a treble twenty, but you are not going to win any prizes.

The smart questions are;

1. Why do we want people to go to the website?

2. What do we want them to do next?

The answer to the first question might be obvious to those of you who sell online. The answer you will say is 'We want them to buy'. This will take care of the small percentage of visitors who are ready and in a position to 'buy now'. But what about the other visitors?

1. The prospects that are researching a purchase.

2. The wife that wants to recommend a purchase to her husband.

3. The customer who is trying to find some repair information, but is considering an upgrade.

All these type of visitors can go in the 'Warm leads' bucket, and the BIG mistake most companies make is thinking that these leads will turn into 'Hot leads' on their own and will miraculously pick their business to buy from.

What you need to start thinking of is the website as the first step in a sales funnel. A sales funnel is designed to automatically turn these 'Warm Leads' into ready to buy 'Hot Leads'. So that when the buying time is here you already have a good relationship with the customer.

So how do you start a sales funnel? You create addictive and sticky data capture tools on your website that highlights a potential buyer's interest, and then starts an automated follow up routine. This will carefully feed the potential buyer with relevant information that they need and are interested in. Here are some simple ways to start the process;

- A custom quote tool that emails the bespoke quote to the enquirer
- A free information pack on their topic of interest automatically emailed to them
- A 'what's right for your tool' that creates some valuable advice based on their answer to some probing questions.

Once you have their emails you can start your sales funnel and be warming up the leads 24/7 without your sales team having to lift a finger.

MARKETING

At the time of this writing the country and the world for that matter are in a fairly serious economic downturn that seems to be taking forever to climb out of. At the same time more and more people are starting small local businesses to make ends meet or to realize a dream they have had for some time but for whatever reason did not act on it. In this section we'll be covering the impact that small businesses have on our economy and why the internet is one of the most cost effective forms of marketing for small businesses.

Why Marketing For Small Business Is Critical

Here are some powerful statistics that should tell you why advertising for your business is not only important but critical at this point in time. According to the United States Small Business Administration (SBA) small businesses make up ninety nine point seven percent, create more than fifty percent of the non farm private gross domestic product in the US. Small businesses employ over fifty percent of all private sector workers and make up ninety seven percent of exporters. There are over five hundred thousand small businesses that start up every year and twenty five percent will be thriving four years later and will create more that seventy five percent of the net new jobs that add to the economy. Due to the economic downturn many people that have been downsized or laid off are starting businesses according a USA Today article "Recession, layoffs fuel many to start small businesses". What this means is that marketing for small businesses is not only very important but critical in order to help pull ourselves out of the economic downturn.

I Already Know Marketing For Small Business Is Important, Now

What Do I Do?

This is where we get into the real cool part about how online marketing can be very cost effective. While the internet is very large and vast and a little misunderstood, it is a great asset when used in marketing for small businesses. Starting with your web presence or your website, you have a twenty four hour presence to the world that can start to create relationships with your potential clients.

How To Use Internet Marketing Correctly

Where a lot of businesses drop the ball is that they don't make the website work for them very well in terms of developing that relationship. You as a business owner can be generating leads by simply setting up an opt in box on your website to collect contact information and let your potential customers learn more about your products and services as well as offer discounts and invite them to events. Utilizing the power of social networking is also an important and cost effective way of marketing simply setting up a like page or fanpage on Facebook opens your presence up to another five hundred million people that spend at least thirty minutes a day on this giant social networking site. Here again is a great way to get your brand in front of potential customers mostly by word of mouth, the best kind of marketing for any business.

Developing long term relationships with people on their terms and offering them products and services that will help them in their daily life is what marketing is all about. The internet has cleared the playing field for anyone operating a small business and is quickly becoming the most cost effective form of marketing for small businesses.

RUN ADS

Advertising is indispensable in sustainable business, however if not done correctly, it may prove very expensive especially for small businesses. Here are some Tips on Effective Advertising for Small Businesses.

- Advert Design

Designing an advert that easily captures the attention of the targeted consumers is the key. Pass the intended message clearly and effectively. Do not put too much into the ad, avoid cluttering at all cost. Expensive ad, with poor design is not effective at all. Come up with an ad that will not only easily attract attention of the potential consumers, but maintain their attention long enough to get intended message.

- Establish Brand

New business first aim is to create awareness of their existence and their products. Do not create persuasive or reminder ads until you have created a higher level of brand awareness. Establishing a brand is usually the tougher assignment compared to persuasive or reminder advertising. It can be even more difficult when you are competing with well established brands.

- Medium selection

Once the ad message is properly prepared, select the suitable medium while considering available budget. You can use TV, radio, Magazines, internet, newspaper among others. Internet and newspaper advertising are affordable especially for new businesses.

Using internet advertising provides extra tools that cannot be used in other ads. You can place as much details as possible, including products details, prices, business locations, and platform for customers to enquire more.

Television, radio, newspaper, magazine and billboard advertisement can however be used to encourage clients to access the websites. They can be very effective in directing consumers to business website.

CONCLUSION

As soon as you determine that a lot of the great benefits that you thought went hand in hand with owning your own small business are myths, the next step is to consider a few factors that might significantly impact the ultimate success of your business plan. It is crucial that you have a solid support system backing you up including a spouse, members of your family, or trusted friends that will help to encourage you and even pitch in when times are tough. Before you even get started you need to guarantee that you have business contacts that can supply solid advice and help you with promotion and marketing when the time comes. Possessing some great financial assets are also crucial as you start and develop this business so you can pay your bills and stay afloat as it grows in the early stages of development.

Get ready for set backs and disappointments that will most likely happen in the first few months, if you are not financially stable enough to make it through early problems, you should not even start a small business. You need to honestly and clearly be able to see the big picture of your situation in order to make it through the vital start up phase so you can stay motivated, focused, and financially able to make it through it all to achieve success.

RESOURCES

Chapter 1. Domain Name

https://tinyurl.com/y8aacuba

Chapter 2. Email

https://tinyurl.com/yd2m7as9

Chapter 3. Phone

https://tinyurl.com/y9og3oey

Chapter 4. Logo

https://tinyurl.com/yd6pnt5m

Chapter 5. Business Cards

https://www.vistaprint.com

Chapter 6. Web Host

https://tinyurl.com/ybnrhlm2

Chapter 7. Website

https://tinyurl.com/yd6pnt5m

Chapter 8. Sales Funnel

https://tinyurl.com/ybf7ch6n

Chapter 9. Marketing

https://tinyurl.com/ybtjok5f

Chapter 10. Run Ads

https://tinyurl.com/y8rus73k

www.ingramcontent.com/pod-product-compliance
Lightning Source LLC
Chambersburg PA
CBHW021349060726
47591CB00006B/2234